Saint Isaac Jogues

Saint Isaac Jogues

With Burning Heart

Written by
Christine Virginia Orfeo, FSP

and

Mary Elizabeth Tebo, FSP

Illustrated by
Barbara Kiwak

Pauline
BOOKS & MEDIA
Boston

Library of Congress Cataloging-in-Publication Data

Orfeo, Christine Virginia.

Saint Isaac Jogues : with burning heart / written by Christine Virginia Orfeo and Mary Elizabeth Tebo ; illustrated by Barbara Kiwak.

p. cm.—(Encounter the saints series)

Summary: A biography of Isaac Jogues, a French Jesuit priest who worked as a Catholic missionary among the native peoples of New France until he was martyred in 1646.

ISBN 0-8198-7063-3 (pbk.)

1. Jogues, Isaac, Saint, 1607-1646—Juvenile literature. 2. Christian saints—New France—Biography—Juvenile literature. [1. Jogues, Isaac, Saint, 1607-1646. 2. Saints.] I. Tebo, Mary Elizabeth. II. Kiwak, Barbara, ill. III. Title. IV. Series.

BX4700.J564 O74 2002

272'.9'092—dc21

2002004324

Printed and published in the U.S.A. by Pauline Books & Media, 50 Saint Pauls Avenue, Boston, MA 02130-3491.

www.pauline.org

Pauline Books & Media is the publishing house of the Daughters of St. Paul, an international congregation of women religious serving the Church with the communications media.

1 2 3 4 5 6   07 06 05 04 03 02

Encounter the Saints Series

Blesseds Jacinta and
Francisco Marto
Shepherds of Fatima

Journeys with Mary
Apparitions of Our Lady

Saint Anthony
of Padua
Fire and Light

Saint Bernadette
Soubirous
Light in the Grotto

Saint Edith Stein
Blessed by the Cross

Saint Elizabeth
Ann Seton
Daughter of America

Saint Francis
of Assisi
Gentle Revolutionary

Saint Ignatius
of Loyola
*For the Greater
Glory of God*

Saint Isaac Jogues
With Burning Heart

Saint Joan of Arc
God's Soldier

Saint Juan Diego
*And Our Lady of
Guadalupe*

Saint Julie Billiart
The Smiling Saint

Saint Maximilian
Kolbe
Mary's Knight

Saint Pio
of Pietrelcina
Rich in Love

For other children's titles on the Saints,
visit our Web site: www.pauline.org

Contents

1

A MIND OF HIS OWN

While the city of Orléans, France, slept soundly under a fresh blanket of snow, most of the Jogues family was wide awake. Long before dawn on that morning of January 10, 1607, lamps burned brightly and there was much commotion in the house. A third son had just been born to the wealthy merchant Laurent Jogues and his wife Françoise. They named the child Isaac.

Right from the start, his mother felt a special love for her little Isaac. He was a happy and quiet baby. *In some mysterious way, it seems that Isaac is more a part of me than my older boys, François and Jacques,* Madame Jogues told herself. As she watched him grow year by year, a thought kept coming back to her: *I believe Isaac will be a priest.*

One day, when Isaac was almost eleven, his father called for him. "Up until now you've studied with a tutor, Isaac," Monsieur Jogues began. "But the Fathers of the Society of Jesus have opened a school here in Orléans. These Jesuits, as they're called, staff some of the finest schools in all of France. I'm going to enroll you in their college, Isaac," his father finished with a smile. (In those days, schools did not follow the same age divisions that they do today.)

At first Isaac was a little worried. He had heard about the long list of rules at this new school: no telling lies, no writing on the desks or walls, no bragging or acting better than others, no talking during times of silence. The students were also required to attend Mass and go to confession on certain days. It seemed strict. But if his parents wanted to enroll him, Isaac would try his best.

Through the years Isaac became a good student and a gracious young man. He was tall for his age and his long legs helped him run faster than any of his classmates. On the other hand, Isaac's light skin and refined features made him look much younger than he really was—something he didn't like at all!

The Jogues family was one of the most respected in the city of Orléans. "Isaac has a promising future ahead of him," friends and relatives were always telling his father. "Maybe he'll turn out to be a merchant or a lawyer." Laurent Jogues would proudly nod his head in agreement.

But Isaac had plans of his own. He enjoyed spending time with the Jesuit priests at his school. He was attracted by their good example and their dedication to God and those in need. As far back as he could remember, Isaac had always loved to receive the sacraments and to slip into church for some quiet prayer. By the time the seventeen-year-old had finished college, his mind was made up: *I'm going to be a priest.*

Some family members and friends were shocked at his decision, but not his mother. (Isaac's father had died a few years earlier.) Madame Jogues was happy. For years she had secretly prayed for Isaac's vocation. The surprise was not that Isaac wanted to be a priest, but that he wanted to be a *Jesuit* priest.

"Why don't you become a diocesan priest here in Orléans, Isaac, near your family?" his mother urged. "If you become a Jesuit, you could be sent anywhere. Your life might even be in danger. Please, Isaac, think about this…" Madame Jogues pleaded, cupping his face in her hands. "We might never see one another again…."

"I have thought about it, Mother, and for a long time," Isaac answered quietly. "I'm certain that God wants me to be a Jesuit and a missionary. I only want what God wants. You understand, don't you?"

"Yes," she whispered.

2

A New Home

The impatient stagecoach driver paced back and forth while Isaac said his final goodbyes to the family. Isaac gave his mother's tearstained cheek one last kiss, then turned and jumped into the carriage. He waved farewell until the last familiar figure was out of sight. It was October of 1624. Isaac, not yet eighteen years old, was on his way to the Jesuit novitiate in Rouen.

After a few days of travel, the stagecoach pulled to a sharp stop in front of the Jesuit College of Rouen. Isaac hopped out. The driver swung the luggage down from the top of the coach and then rumbled on. For a moment Isaac just stood there. He gazed up at the sprawling building surrounded by high walls. How different it was from his home! The teenager fought back an unexpected feeling of panic.

Summoning his courage, Isaac picked up his bags and approached the front entrance. He knocked. In what seemed like just a few seconds, the heavy door creaked open. A porter led Isaac into a dim, simply furnished parlor. He left him waiting there.

Some minutes later, Isaac heard footsteps approaching. A friendly, young-looking priest entered the room. "Isaac!" he greeted him warmly. "Welcome to Rouen and to the Society of Jesus! I'm Father Louis Lalemant, the master of novices."

"Thank you, Father. I'm happy and grateful to be here," Isaac responded with a smile.

From his first days in the novitiate, Isaac felt right at home. He adapted quickly and was peaceful in his new Jesuit life of prayer, work, and study. Deep in his heart, his desire to be a missionary continued to grow. It was like a fire that couldn't be extinguished. Soon it dominated all his thoughts and prayers.

"Father Louis, please let me volunteer to go to a mission country!" Isaac begged.

"You must accept as God's will whatever work you will be given," the wise novice master replied. Father Louis knew just how Isaac felt. Years earlier he too had petitioned his superiors to send him to the missions. But his dream had never been fulfilled. His talents had been put to use in other ways.

France had begun to establish colonies in New France, the area we call Canada today, around the year 1603. As colonies were set up, French missionary priests traveled to New France to minister to the Catholic colonists and preach the Gospel to the native people.

In 1625, Jesuit Fathers Charles Lalemant, John de Brébeuf, and Ennemond Massé passed through the Rouen novitiate on their way to the city of Dieppe. From there they would set sail for New France.

Meeting these missionaries stirred up Isaac's enthusiasm once again. "Father, please accept me for the missions," he pleaded with his novice master.

"Where do you feel called to work, Isaac?"

"Constantinople! That's where I should go—to work among the people of the East."

Father Louis was thoughtful for a moment. "Brother Isaac," he said quietly, "New France is where you will die."

Isaac pronounced his religious vows as a Jesuit on October 24, 1626, placing his whole life in God's hands with great joy. A few days later, he was sent to study at the College of La Fléche. During the three years he spent there, he never gave up asking his superiors to send him to the missions. But at La Fléche Isaac began thinking more and more about New France. Many of his fellow Jesuit students dreamed of being sent there as missionaries. They traded stories about the heroic Jesuits already working there.

Once he finished his studies at the College of La Fléche, Isaac, who was almost twenty-three by then, received a new assignment. For four years he taught grammar to young boys at the Jesuit College of Rouen. Next he was called to the College of Clermont in Paris. This was exciting! At Clermont he would finally begin his theological studies for the priesthood.

Brother Isaac had always found schoolwork easy enough. But the theology courses needed for ordination turned out to be a real challenge. Isaac's desire to become a priest gave him the courage to go on. It didn't bother him that he wasn't at the head of his class. All he wanted was to be able to instruct others in the Catholic faith and lead them to God. All he wanted was to become a good and holy servant of God.

"Are you willing to go to New France, Isaac?"

TO NEW FRANCE

At the beginning of January 1636, Isaac received a surprise.

His superior informed him that he would be ordained months before the expected date. But this was not all. "There is an urgent need for priests and brothers in New France," Father Estienne Binet confided. "We'd like to send you there after your ordination, Isaac. This is why you will be ordained early. Are you willing to go?"

Isaac couldn't believe his ears. "Father," he said, trying to control his excitement, "I've prayed to go to the missions for years. Of course I'll go! And very willingly!"

Ordination day soon arrived. During the Mass Isaac prostrated himself before the altar of the college chapel. His heart was pounding with joy. Rising to his knees, he felt the bishop's strong hands press upon his head. He heard the bishop offering special prayers. Other priests stepped forward to vest Isaac with the stole and chasuble. The bishop then anointed the palms of his hands with sacred chrism. Its sweet-scented aroma filled the sanctuary. Isaac Jogues was now a priest forever!

Françoise Jogues' joy over her son's ordination was mixed with sorrow when she learned that Isaac would soon be leaving for New France. Father Isaac traveled back to Orléans, his hometown, to celebrate his first Mass. On that day Madame Jogues had the indescribable happiness of receiving Holy Communion from her son. That happiness would strengthen her for many years to come.

After his short visit to Orléans, Father Isaac returned to Rouen to await his assignment. Finally, the summons came: "Go to Dieppe and sail for New France with the first ships heading out."

On April 8, 1636, Isaac boarded a ship in the fleet of eight departing for New France. He stood by the rail watching the horizon of France grow more and more distant. The waves slapped against the ship's sides, sending up a salty spray. *My God, I've never been so happy!* the young priest prayed. *Strengthen me to bring your Gospel to the people of New France. I offer you everything for them—everything.*

The stormy voyage lasted eight weeks. Toward the end of this time, the small French fleet began to split up, with each ship heading for its own destination. On June 2, an excited cry finally arose from the lookout of Father Isaac's ship: "Land! Land up ahead!"

Isaac rushed to the deck. He gazed on New France for the first time, eagerly taking in the sights and sounds of the island of St. Louis de Miscou to which they were drawing near. Rowboats hurried out to meet the ship. They would ferry the passengers to land. Closer to the shoreline, roughly fashioned canoes dotted the deep blue bay. These were paddled by some of the native men. Shouts of welcome filled the air.

As the anchor was dropped and the rowboats came closer, Isaac spotted the happiest sight of all—two young Jesuits waving enthusiastically from the shore. They were Father Charles Du Marché and Father Charles Turgis, two of Isaac's former classmates. As soon as Isaac jumped from the rowboat, they threw their arms around him in a hearty welcome. "How good it is to see you again, Isaac! Welcome! Welcome to New France!"

The excited priests finally led Isaac up a hill to their log cabin. There the three Jesuits knelt before the Blessed Sacrament and thanked God for Father Isaac's safe journey.

Afterward, huddled around the fire in the cabin, they feasted on fish, acorns, and various fruits and talked for hours about France and their friends back home. It had been a whole year since Fathers Du Marché and Turgis had received any news from France. And they were full of questions!

Later that afternoon, the three priests walked around the small settlement named after Saint Charles.

Father Isaac eagerly observed the Algonquin Indians who had come to the mission to trade furs for goods brought by the French. The native men had high cheekbones, copper-colored skin and straight black hair. Their speech was what fascinated Isaac the most. *It's like nothing I've ever heard,* he marveled.

Two weeks after Father Isaac's arrival at the St. Charles Mission, he and Father Du Marché rowed their boat up the St. Lawrence River to the French settlement at Quebec. They moored the boat and hiked up a muddy road to the Jesuit residence of

Notre Dame des Anges (Our Lady of the Angels). There at Notre Dame Father Isaac celebrated his first Mass in New France. Afterward he received an energetic greeting from the Jesuit fathers and brothers stationed at the mission.

Isaac later wrote to his mother: "I don't know what it is like to enter heaven, but I know it would be difficult to experience a joy greater than when I set foot in New France and celebrated my first Mass here. I felt as if it were Christmas and that I was born to a new life in God!"

4

THREE RIVERS

Father Paul Le Jeune, superior of the Jesuit community and the French missions in New France, arrived to greet Isaac later that morning. The two priests soon settled down to talk.

"The number of settlers in New France is growing beyond all expectations," Father Paul explained. "It's remarkable to see the enthusiasm with which the colonists build their settlements."

"But what about the native people?" Father Isaac broke in. "Are they being cared for? It is their land, after all, that we are building on."

Father Paul gave Isaac an understanding look. "Fathers Charles Garnier and Pierre Chastellain left two days ago to begin working with the Hurons," he replied. "I don't know if I can spare you right now, Isaac. The French colonists here need priests too. But when it becomes possible, I promise that you will be the next missionary to leave for the Huron villages."

"That is my greatest desire, Father," Isaac confided.

"I know," the superior answered with a knowing smile. "In the meantime I'd like you to help out in Quebec."

Father Isaac didn't have long to wait for his desire to be fulfilled. In a few weeks he received a letter from Father Paul. "The Hurons have accepted Father Pierre and Father Charles," the superior reported. "A fleet of their canoes carrying furs to trade is on its way to Three Rivers right now. It should be arriving soon. We're hoping the Huron braves will be willing to take you back with them, Isaac. Come immediately to Three Rivers!"

Father Isaac headed out of Quebec on the next boat. Father Paul was on hand to welcome him when he disembarked at Three Rivers. Waiting excitedly on the shore was another familiar figure: Father Jacques Buteux—Isaac's former classmate. "Welcome, Isaac!" Jacques cried, warmly taking Isaac by the shoulders. "Look at you! A missionary at last!"

"At last!" Isaac happily repeated.

"You must come and see our newest building," Father Jacques urged as he and

Father Paul led the way. "It's a combination residence and chapel. We've called it Notre Dame de l'Immaculate Conception (Our Lady of the Immaculate Conception)."

Father Isaac gazed up at the large, plain building with admiration. "Ahh…Jacques…it's beautiful, truly it is!"

The next few days were filled with anticipation. Three Rivers was a post at which the Hurons traded goods with the French each year. To reach the settlement, the Hurons needed to travel down the Ottawa and St. Maurice Rivers. Unfortunately, the Algonquin Indians, who controlled the Ottawa River, were envious of the Hurons. As a result, they demanded that the Hurons pay a high toll for their use of the Ottawa. Would the Algonquins even allow the Huron fleet through? The Jesuits wondered.

Finally, on August 13, a Huron canoe arrived. "More of our men will come soon," the Huron chief explained to the priests.

The next day Three Rivers was in an uproar. Instead of Huron canoes it was a cluster of Algonquin canoes that paddled into port. Hanging from tall poles in the canoes were twenty-eight Iroquois scalps that fluttered menacingly in the wind. The Algonquin warriors chanted songs of victory as they pulled their vessels to shore.

In one of the bark canoes a captive Iroquois man and woman stood singing in defiance. As soon as the Iroquois brave stepped onto the beach, Algonquin women and children bounded toward him. They beat him with clubs and heavy ropes. They pressed pieces of burning wood against his skin. Some of the Algonquin braves then bit the prisoner's arms and legs.

Father Paul rushed into the screaming mob. "Stop! Stop this!" he shouted. "If you don't, we won't help you with food and clothing."

One by one the Algonquins backed away from their victim. The braves finally pushed both prisoners back into a canoe. They would be taken to an Algonquin camp where the torture would be completed.

The whole episode sickened Father Isaac. Father Paul had warned him about the treatment of prisoners among the Indians, but Isaac hadn't been prepared for this. "Sometimes they speak and act with great wisdom, giving evidence of their keen intelligence," the Jesuit superior had explained. "At other times they are incredibly superstitious and can be merciless and cruel."

They truly don't know any better, Isaac thought. *If only we could open their minds and hearts to Jesus and his Gospel…*

. It could change everything.

In the early morning of August 19, the rest of the Huron canoes finally crowded the St. Lawrence River. In the lead vessel stood a thin, bearded man waving his paddle in greeting.

Isaac strained to get a better glimpse of him. *Could it be Father Daniel? No!* he immediately thought. *It's not possible! He looks nothing like him.*

But it was! Father Antoine Daniel—a Jesuit who had lived among the Hurons for four long years—had returned.

The priests waded into the water and eagerly pulled Father Antoine's canoe ashore. They embraced the fragile-looking missionary with great emotion. "Antoine! Finally you've come! It's been so long…."

The priest's skin was rough and his cheeks sunken. What was left of his threadbare cassock was in shreds. His breviary hung from a cord around his neck. His time among the Hurons had reduced this once robust man to a mere skeleton.

Isaac could only stare at Father Antoine in awe. But even as he watched, he prayed, *My God, let me take his place!*

5

AMONG THE HURONS

The following days were filled with meetings between the French blackrobes (the name the Indians gave the Jesuits) and the Hurons. During the farewell feast preceding the Hurons' departure, the Huron chief of Ossossané squatted beside Father Antoine. "Why don't you send a blackrobe to live in our village? Do you love us less than the others?"

"My brother," the priest replied, "a blackrobe greatly desires to stay with you."

"Then tell him to come!" the chief exclaimed.

This was the invitation Father Isaac had been waiting for!

Isaac didn't have many belongings to pack. But he did spend long hours on his knees before the Blessed Sacrament thanking God for this grace and begging for the strength he would need. It would be several weeks before he could celebrate Mass again, receive Holy Communion, and be absolved of his sins in the Sacrament of Penance.

Father Isaac also learned from the other missionaries the proper way of behaving among the native people. The Hurons expected the blackrobes to work hard, eat little, and show no signs of fatigue. "Just remember that you need to remain calm and cheerful no matter what happens," Father Paul advised him.

Before leaving Three Rivers with Father Isaac, the Hurons held a feast in his honor. At this celebration they accepted him as a brother into their nation. The Indians soon discovered, however, that they couldn't pronounce Isaac's name. "You have a sharp eye and are very quick," some of the braves observed. "We will give you a new name, a Huron name. You are *Ondessonk*, Bird of Prey."

Isaac smiled and nodded in approval. *Ondessonk*, he repeated to himself. *Ondessonk!*

The French government hoped to strengthen its ties with the Indians by allowing some French children to live in the native villages while welcoming some of the native children into the French settlements. A young French boy named Jean Amyot was to accompany Father Isaac. Jean was expected to learn the Huron language and

Father Jacques traced the sign of the cross over Isaac.

customs. The French officials hoped that later on he could serve as an interpreter.

On Sunday, August 24, Father Isaac strode through the wet morning grass to the waiting Huron canoes. Jean ran on ahead.

"I can see you're anxious to go, Jean," Isaac chuckled.

"Yes, Father!" the boy exclaimed.

A Huron brave signaled for Isaac to climb into his canoe. Isaac carefully took up his position, trying not to upset the delicate balance of the birch-bark vessel. Isaac looked back at the priests waving from the shore. He bowed his head as Father Jacques's raised hand traced the sign of the cross over him. He was finally on his way to the native villages!

Noiselessly and swiftly the Hurons paddled through the waters. Their keen eyes continually searched the river's edge for signs of their enemy, the Iroquois.

That first day they traveled thirty miles. After a supper of sagamite—powdered corn mixed with water—Father Isaac and Jean slept on the damp ground. Their only shelter was the towering evergreens.

As the grueling trip wore on, Isaac accustomed himself to long hours of squatting in the canoe, burning thirst, and hunger pangs. Up rivers and through lakes the Huron braves expertly guided their canoes. Whenever waterfalls or rocks blocked their path, the Indians pulled up onto the muddy banks and carried their canoes and supplies on their backs. Father Isaac silently helped.

The trip soon proved to be too much for young Jean. He grew so weak from physical exertion and lack of food that Isaac had to carry him. Unsteady on his own feet, Father Isaac was relieved when a Huron agreed to carry Jean in return for having his heavier load of hatchets carried by Father Isaac.

As the canoes neared the Huron village of Ihonatiria, the braves paddled with new energy. Finally, on September 11, the band of canoes slipped into the sheltered cove at the foot of the settlement.

Isaac climbed eagerly out of his canoe. The pain in his back and legs was suddenly forgotten. *Thank you, Lord,* he silently prayed. *Thank you for bringing me here!* Running toward him was the towering figure of Father Jean de Brébeuf—*Echon* to the Indians—the first Jesuit to work among the Hurons. Close behind came Fathers François Le Mercier, Charles Garnier, and Pierre Chastellain. Isaac was suddenly swept up in a tangle of arms while everyone talked and laughed at the same time.

"Isaac, I'd given up hope of receiving any new missionaries this year! Thank God you've come!" Father Jean exclaimed.

The five priests joyfully headed for the bark cabin called St. Joseph's. The cabin was about fifty feet long and eighteen feet wide and was shaped like a tunnel. It had a door at each end, but no windows. Openings cut into the ceiling let out the smoke from fires used for heating and cooking. At one end was the partitioned off chapel. There the priests knelt and thanked the Lord for the safe arrival of Father Isaac and Jean. Next came the happy preparations for a feast of fish, roasted corn, squash, and raisins.

While the priests showed Isaac the cabin, the Hurons stood outside discussing this new blackrobe, Ondessonk.

"He looks like all white men," one brave who had made the canoe trip with Father Isaac declared. "His face has no color and his eyes are blue, but he is strong and does what he is told. He can also run!" the Huron approvingly affirmed.

Groups of curious listeners, eager to get a good look at Isaac, pushed their way into the Jesuits' cabin. Yes! It was just as the brave had said. Ondessonk was no better looking than Echon!

6

GREAT SUFFERING, GREATER JOY

Father Jean de Brébeuf, the superior of the Jesuit community at Ihonatiria, had been a missionary to the Hurons for ten years. He was more fluent in the Huron language than any other white man in New France. He was also taller and stronger than any Huron warrior. For this reason Echon was both loved and feared by the native people.

During his first few days in Ihonatiria, Father Isaac began to build up his strength again. The warm sunshine and clean forest air speeded his recuperation from the exhausting canoe trip. But one morning Isaac felt strangely weak. A violent fever followed. Within days all of the Jesuits except Father Jean, Father Pierre (who had returned from Three Rivers), and Father François fell deathly ill. Influenza had struck Ihonatiria. The Huron braves who had traveled through the infected land of the Algonquins had brought the dreaded disease back with them. *It's a true epidemic!* thought Father Jean. *Lord, have mercy on us!*

Fear swept through the Huron villages as one by one the Indians were overcome by the illness. The native people turned to their sorcerers who performed dances and rituals to ward off the evil spirits they believed were the cause of the illness.

Father Isaac's fever raged out of control. His condition grew so critical that he was at the point of death. He could no longer eat. His continual coughing threatened to choke him. Father Jean knew there was only one chance to save Isaac: they had to release some blood in order to bring his fever down. The question was who could safely make the incision in the vein? Neither Jean, François, nor Pierre had ever done such a thing, and they were all frightened. Father Jean knelt beside Father Isaac. "Isaac, you're dying," he said gently. "Our only hope is to bleed you...."

Isaac heard the anxiety in Father Jean's voice. He understood why his companions feared making the dangerous cut. If it were not done correctly, he would bleed to death. "I'll...do it...myself," Isaac panted. The three priests raised Isaac to a sitting position and Father Jean handed him a small knife. With a trembling hand, Isaac pressed the knife to his arm. The blood flowed out, and he lapsed into a coma. By the next day, however, Father Isaac was conscious again and his fever began to drop. In fact, Isaac was the first Frenchman to recover from the influenza.

As soon as he was well, Father Isaac joined Father Jean and Father Pierre in caring for the stricken Hurons. Every day they faced death—threatened by the native sorcerers and angry Hurons who sometimes blamed the blackrobes for the epidemic. Courageously the priests baptized dying infants. They spoke about God to any of the sick who would listen, and they offered baptism to the adults who were beyond hope of recovery.

The influenza epidemic finally came to an end in February of 1637. Spring cleared the waterways of ice and the snow covering the forest trails melted.

That June, after all their difficult and perilous work among the sick Hurons, the blackrobes received an unexpected grace from God. Tsiouendaentaha, an influential Huron, asked to be baptized.

"For three years I have studied about the God of the blackrobes," he said. "Now I will become his child."

The altar of the priests' chapel was ablaze with candles and decorated with colorful flowers. Tsiouendaentaha was baptized and given the Christian name Peter. He received Holy Communion during the Mass, which was attended by crowds of curious Hurons. A great celebration followed, with Father Jean and Peter both giving speeches. The Jesuits were overjoyed. At last there was a Christian Huron!

7

"Your Prayer Is Heard"

By 1638, Father Isaac and the other priests were doing better with the Huron language. The Hurons loved discussions and storytelling, especially during the long winter months. "We like to listen to you, Ondessonk," they confided to Isaac. The Jesuits tried their best to sow the seed of the Gospel, but there were many setbacks. The Hurons could be cruel to their captured enemies, and many were known for lying, stealing, and immorality. Worst of all were the sorcerers whose superstition and spirit worship held great power over the people.

The priests were slow to baptize the Hurons who asked to become Christians. They wanted to make sure that the native people understood the demands of Christianity—and that they were willing to live up to them. A second Christian Huron lived in the village of Ossossané. His name was Chihwatenhwa, and he was the nephew of a great chief of the Bear Nation. Chihwatenhwa had been baptized and given the name Joseph when he was seriously ill with influenza. He recovered from the disease and became a faithful Catholic. His wife Aonetta and their daughter and sons were later baptized too. Joseph and Aonetta became the first Hurons to celebrate a Christian wedding ceremony. They gave a wonderful example to the other Huron men and women.

But all was not well. Because half of the population of Ihonatiria had died during the influenza epidemic, serious problems arose there. The people had lost much of their hope and the village was deteriorating. The palisade protecting the settlement gradually began to collapse and many of the cabins were beyond repair. The fields no longer produced enough crops to feed the community, and game in the forest had become scarce because of over hunting. "We'll have to move," Father Jean announced to the other priests one day. "We've done all that we could in Ihonatiria. Many of the Hurons are leaving here. We must go where we can reach more people."

After a month of negotiations with the Attigneenongnahcs tribe, the most hostile of the Hurons, the blackrobes were allowed to move into the village of Teanaustayaé.

There were many wars between the Hurons and the Iroquois during that summer of 1638. The next year, the Jesuits managed to build a new house fifteen miles north of Teanaustayaé. They called it Sainte Marie.

Just when everything seemed to be settling down, an epidemic of smallpox broke out and spread through the Huron villages. Once again the blackrobes walked from village to village caring for the sick. They were always in danger of the sorcerers who tried to turn the people against them. While tending the sick, the priests also took a careful census of the Indian villages and drew the first maps of southern New France.

A new spirit of openness to the Gospel brought more converts to the faith. By 1642 there were 120 adult Huron Christians.

The most outstanding convert of all was Ahatsistari, the greatest of all Huron chiefs. So incredible were his war victories that he was a legend among the Huron tribes.

On Holy Saturday, 1642, Chief Ahatsistari was baptized and given the name Eustace.

Father Isaac shared in the great joy of the celebration. But he was restless. *What about the many others who don't yet know you, my Lord?* he prayed. *How can I bring them your Gospel?*

One afternoon, when the village chapel was empty, Isaac knelt in prayer. Deep within his heart he felt a tremendous desire to suffer for God, to endure anything in order to bring God's Word to as many of the Indians as possible. *Please, Lord,* he begged, bowing until his head touched the altar step, *take me. I offer you my life for the salvation of these people. Please...take me.* A strong sensation of heat ran through his body. It was as if the love burning in his heart had been released. Father Isaac waited and listened for an answer from God. In the peaceful stillness, words came into his mind. They were repeated over and over again so that he could never forget them: *Your prayer is heard. What you have asked for will be done. Be comforted. Be strong-hearted.*

Isaac had no doubt that it was God who had spoken to him. "Yes, my Lord," he whispered. "I'm in your hands. Whatever happens, I'm in your hands."

8

"I'm Willing…"

The year 1642 turned out to be a dangerous one for the Hurons. Never before had the Iroquois—members of the Mohawk Indian nation—been so fierce in their raids against them. Although the Hurons were less war-like than the Iroquois, they would not back down when attacked.

The Dutch, like the French, were trying to establish colonies in the New World. The Dutch settlers, who traded with the Iroquois, supplied them with muskets. But the French colonists, who traded with the Hurons, refused to give the Hurons arms and ammunition. They were afraid the Indians might use these to attack their own communities.

That June the Huron chiefs planned another trading expedition with the French in Quebec. Frightening rumors spread through the Huron villages. "The Iroquois are planning to ambush us as we travel to Quebec!" the braves murmured. "It will be a dangerous journey!"

Despite the danger, the Hurons decided to make the trip. Food and supplies from Three Rivers and Quebec were needed for the long winter ahead. A priest was also required to go on the expedition. Letters had to be delivered and reports made to the Jesuit superiors in Quebec. Instructions, letters, medicine, and equipment had to be brought back to the mission.

Father Jerome Lalemant, the superior of the Sainte Marie mission at that time, felt tormented over the decision he had to make. *I'm endangering the life of any priest I send with the Hurons,* he thought. After much prayer, Father Jerome finally called Father Isaac. "Isaac, I want you to understand that I'm not commanding," the superior explained. "I'm only asking if you'd be willing to go on the trip to Quebec. You realize the serious risks involved...."

In his heart, Isaac heard again the mysterious words: *Your prayer is heard. What you have asked for will be done....* "Yes, Father, I'm aware of the dangers," Father Isaac calmly replied. "And I'm willing to go... very willing."

William Coûture was a French layman who had dedicated his life to helping the Jesuits in the Indian missions. William and other volunteers like him were called *donnés.* William also accepted Father Jerome's invitation to make the trip to Quebec.

Eustace Ahatsistari, the famous Huron chief and Christian convert, led the traveling party. The voyage was a tense one. But after a month of traveling, the small fleet of four canoes safely reached Three Rivers.

Isaac spent a few days in Three Rivers ordering some supplies. Then he journeyed on to Quebec. There were no signs of any Iroquois along the way. In Quebec, Isaac made the necessary reports about the Huron mission to Father Barthélmy Vimont, the Jesuit superior of New France.

"Isaac," Father Barthélmy confided, "I think it's necessary to send someone with medical training back with you to Sainte Marie. There is a donné whom I think would be very happy to go. He's been working here in our hospital. His name is René Goupil. When he was younger, René joined our Society in France. After some months as a novice he was forced to leave because of poor health. He then studied medicine. When his physical condition improved, René applied to become a donné and was accepted. He has always loved our Jesuit way of life."

"I'd be honored to have him join us in Sainte Marie," Isaac responded enthusiastically.

"Good. I'll talk with him," Father Barthélmy concluded. "I want to make it very clear to him that this is a dangerous mission, and that he's completely free to say yes or no."

9

AMBUSH!

"Of course I'll go to Sainte Marie!" René exclaimed. "You know how long I've wished to work among the Hurons, Father Barthélmy. Thank you for this opportunity!"

On July 28, Father Isaac, William, and René left Quebec with several Hurons. They reached Three Rivers two days later. Isaac was overjoyed to be able to celebrate Mass there on July 31, the feast of Saint Ignatius of Loyola, the founder of the Jesuits.

News soon reached Three Rivers that the Iroquois warriors had left the area. It seemed that they had been frightened away by the arrival of some large French ships. If they wished to have a safe trip back to the Huron villages, Father Isaac, his helpers, and the Hurons would have to leave as soon as possible. Everyone rushed to pack their belongings and the supplies.

Just after dawn on the morning of August 1, Eustace Ahatsistari, Father Isaac, and the rest of the group squatted on the damp ground for the traditional Indian council held before a journey. There were now forty members in the traveling party, since more Hurons had asked to return to Sainte Marie. Twelve canoes were ready to carry them home.

In turn, each of the Indians spoke. Finally, Eustace, their leader, stood. "My brothers," he began, "if I fall into the hands of the Iroquois, I cannot hope to live. I will tell them the French have come to tell us of eternal life and of a God who made everything. I will tell them of a heaven for those who honor God and of a hell for those who do not. They may torture my body, but they cannot take away my hope of heaven."

All the Christian Hurons expressed their agreement. Father Isaac silently thanked God for Eustace's great faith and example.

At the end of their first day of travel, they had to choose between two possible routes. One would take them into the open waters of the St. Lawrence River; the other would bring them between the mainland and some of the surrounding islands. The first route was longer, but it would protect them from ambush. The second route was shorter, but extremely dangerous. It would keep the canoes close to shore where the

Iroquois might be hiding. The Hurons decided to take the second route.

After camping for the night, all woke before dawn. The travelers ate their breakfast of sagamite quickly. Father Isaac then led the group in a hushed prayer. Within minutes they were back at their paddles, gliding through the water.

In a short while the canoes came to a swamp covered with weeds and tall grass. As they approached a passage between two islands, the waterway became narrower. The Huron canoes fell into single file.

Suddenly, war cries broke the silence. Iroquois warriors, streaked with blood-red paint, emerged from the grass. Musket shots whizzed through the air. Arrows shot back from the canoes.

Above the confusion Eustace cried out, "Great God, I look to you for help!"

Father Isaac got to his knees, making the sign of the cross over the Hurons and Frenchmen as he shouted the words of absolution.

Just then, Atieronhonk, the leader of Father Isaac's canoe, was injured by a musket shot. Atieronhonk had never been baptized.

Isaac bent over him and asked, "Do you wish to be baptized?"

"Yes, Ondessonk! Do it before we are captured or killed!"

Father Isaac cupped his hands in the river and poured water over Atieronhonk's head. "I baptize you Bernard in the name of the Father, and of the Son, and of the Holy Spirit. Amen."

Their canoe abruptly ran aground, throwing Isaac into tall grass which concealed him from view. From his hiding place he watched and prayed in agony as the Hurons were overcome one by one. As a priest, he couldn't join in the fighting. *I could escape,* he thought, *the Iroquois haven't seen me, and I'm a fast runner. But I could never abandon our Frenchmen or the Hurons. They need a priest now more than ever!*

Isaac jumped to his feet. With his arms raised in surrender, he walked toward the closest Iroquois. "Don't be afraid!" he said. "Take me prisoner!"

10

TRAIL OF PAIN

The warrior looked at Father Isaac in disbelief. Overcoming his shock, he threw himself at Isaac, knocking him to the ground. Within seconds, other Iroquois braves were on top of him. They beat him and tore off his habit. Yanking him to his feet, they made him join the rest of the prisoners. One brave began to tie Isaac's feet together. "You don't need to do that," he said calmly. "The French and the Hurons are the bonds that will keep me as your prisoner. I will never leave them!"

All of the prisoners had been badly beaten. René was so tightly tied to the ground that he couldn't move. Father Isaac bent down and embraced him. "My brother," he whispered, "we can't understand why this has happened. But God is our Lord and Master. He knows what is best."

"Father," René answered, "blessed be God. He has permitted this. May his will be done."

As Isaac walked among the captives, encouraging them to trust in God and not to lose hope, wild shouts of victory echoed through the forest. More warriors stepped into the clearing leading their greatest prize—Eustace Ahatsistari. Father Isaac grasped Eustace by his bleeding shoulders, but the Iroquois wrenched him away.

Isaac's eyes searched the group of prisoners. William Coûture was not among them. Had he escaped? *Let it be so!* Isaac prayed. William had, in fact, escaped, and had killed one of the Iroquois chiefs. But not wanting to abandon Father Isaac and René, he returned and was captured.

Another band of Iroquois soon appeared at the clearing. Behind them they dragged William, covered with blood. They had beaten him horribly and had pulled out his fingernails. "Be brave, William, my brother and friend," Father Isaac sobbed, as he hugged the wounded man. "The torments in store for us will be terrible, but they will all end. The glory and happiness which will follow in heaven will never end."

"Don't worry...Father," William gasped. "I believe...God...will help me."

The Iroquois misunderstood what was happening. They thought Isaac was congratulating William for having killed their chief. They ripped him away and beat him with clubs and muskets until he fell unconscious on the ground. Other braves pulled out some of his fingernails. They crushed his forefingers with their teeth.

After torturing René in the same way, the Iroquois filled their canoes with the Huron captives and the bounty. They were anxious to return to the safety of their own country.

The days following their ambush brought new tortures to the captives. All except Father Isaac were still bound by tight leather thongs. They were cramped in the narrow canoes, and their exposed skin had no protection against the mosquitoes, flies, gnats, or merciless sun. All their wounds soon became infected.

Father Isaac and René were in the same canoe. On the third or fourth day following the ambush, René spoke in a whisper to Isaac, "Father, God has always inspired me to dedicate my life to him. Until today I was never worthy of this grace. But I desire more than ever to make this offering and to pronounce my vows in the Society of Jesus."

Isaac had to hold back his tears of joy and admiration. "Yes, René," he managed to whisper back. "There is nothing to prevent me from receiving your vows in the name of Father Provincial."

In a low voice, René pronounced the vows he had longed to make years before. Father Isaac blessed him. They were now Jesuit brothers. They would encourage and strengthen each other in the days ahead.

A few days later, an Iroquois brought good news. Another group of 200 of their braves was camped on an island, only a day's journey away. The Iroquois were thrilled. They could stop at this camp to replenish their food supply and show off their prisoners!

When the Iroquois and their captives arrived at the island, the air filled with shrieks of triumph. The French and Huron prisoners were thrown from their canoes into the shallow water. The waiting group of Iroquois warriors lunged at them, beating them fiercely. The original Iroquois captors had to rescue their prisoners from the angry mob, in order to save them for the next form of torture.

The 200 Iroquois warriors now picked up sticks, clubs, and thorny branches. They faced each other in two rows that stretched up the side of a small hill rising from the shore. Father Isaac looked to the top of the hill. He could see a crude platform made of branches. Isaac knew now what was coming. He had been told about this.... He closed his eyes. *My God,* he prayed, *help us! We're going to run the gauntlet....*

The prisoners were stripped of their clothes and forced into a single file. The Hurons came first, then the French. Father Isaac, the most valuable prisoner, was last of all. Each of the prisoners was forced to run up the hill between the two rows of screaming Iroquois. As they tried to pass, the braves struck them with clubs, then tripped and beat them again.

Father Isaac could only pray as he watched his friends being tortured. At last it was his turn. He tried to dash up the hill. But it was impossible. Blows pounded him on every side. Isaac finally fell unconscious to the ground. He was dragged to the top of the hill. When he came to, the warriors threw him onto the platform. Some of the braves pressed burning sticks against his arms and legs. Another bit off his thumb. René and William were being tortured in the same way. To stop them from bleeding too much, the Iroquois laid red-hot stones upon their wounds.

The French were finally thrown off the platform, and the Iroquois began to torture their Huron prisoners. When Father Isaac saw the unbelievably cruel things the Iroquois were doing to Eustace Ahatsistari, who stood brave and motionless, he climbed back onto the stage. Isaac wept as he tried to console his friend. The Iroquois thrust him from the platform. A brave grasped Father Isaac's nose, ready to cut it off with the long knife he held. Isaac knew that if this happened, he would be instantly killed. It was the custom of the Indians to kill anyone who had been badly disfigured. *Lord, I offer you my life,* he prayed. The warrior stared into Isaac's calm eyes. He slowly released his hold and lowered the knife. The warrior returned a few minutes later and tried to attack Father Isaac a second time. But the same mysterious force again held him back. The brave finally walked away in bewilderment.

11

THE FIRST MARTYR

For days the band of triumphant Iroquois warriors rowed their victims deeper into their territory. Along the way they stopped at various Iroquois camps, forcing the prisoners to run the gauntlet each time. The Hurons and the Frenchmen were exhausted. They were weak from hunger and suffering terribly from their wounds. As their food supply grew smaller, the Iroquois forced the prisoners to walk faster. If they stayed in a village at night, boys and girls threw burning coals at the prisoners.

One night, after they reached a village, a council of Iroquois war chiefs met to discuss the fate of their captives. They decided to divide the prisoners among the villages. Some Hurons were destined to be tortured and executed. Father Isaac and René were to become slaves of the Iroquois village chief at Ossernenon. William was given to an Iroquois family living in the village of Tionontoguen.

Ossernenon was a village of about forty longhouses. A tall fence of stakes hewn from tree trunks surrounded it. Father Isaac and René were allowed to rest during their first days in the village. Little by little their wounds began to heal.

The Dutch settlement of Rensselaerswyck was about forty miles from Ossernenon. When Arendt Van Corlaer, the leader of the colony, heard that Isaac, René, and William had been captured by the Iroquois, he hurried to Ossernenon.

"We wish to buy the Frenchmen from you," he told the Iroquois chiefs. "All the goods and supplies I have brought will be yours if you give them to us."

"We will do all that we can to please our Dutch friends," an Iroquois spokesman answered. "But we cannot do what you are asking!"

Van Corlaer had to return to Rensselaerswyck—without Isaac, René, and William.

Isaac and René spent their days praying the rosary and helping the women harvest corn. They lived with many other Iroquois in a longhouse about fifty feet long and twenty feet wide. Down its center burned many small fires that continually filled the house with thick, black smoke. The floor was dirt. With the coming of autumn, the air was damp and cold.

Since Father Isaac had lived with the Hurons for six years, he was familiar with their customs. He could foresee how the native people would react to different situations, and he was skillful in dealing with them. René, who was not used to living with the Indians, had a much harder time adjusting to their way of life. In Ossernenon, René was considered a coward. When the Iroquois saw him praying, they said, "He must be calling down evil spirits upon us!"

"You need to be careful about how you act in front of the Iroquois, René," Isaac repeatedly warned. "They are very superstitious."

One afternoon René was playing with some of the Iroquois children. He lifted one little boy in his arms and placed his hat on the child's head. Then, as he had done so many times with the children in Quebec, René guided the child's hand to make the sign of the cross.

Out of the darkness of the longhouse came a cry of anger. The boy's grandfather had been watching. "You have put an evil spell on the boy!" he screamed, beating René until he was forced to run away.

When Father Isaac learned what had happened, he took René outside the village. They hid in a cluster of trees where they could talk without being seen.

"René, you must be ready for anything now. That old man could have killed you."

"My Father, I am ready for anything as long as I am in the grace of God."

Father Isaac heard René's confession. Then they knelt on the moist ground and prayed for the grace to be faithful to God in the trials ahead.

Father Jogues and René prayed the rosary together on the way back to their longhouse. When they had almost reached Ossernenon, two warriors approached them on the path. They both wore woolen blankets over their folded arms. The tallest of the two braves claimed to be the most powerful man in the Iroquois nation.

"Go back to the village!" he commanded.

Father Isaac sensed danger. "Let us offer ourselves to God and to Mary, our Mother," he whispered to René.

"You walk ahead!" the tallest Iroquois ordered, gesturing to Isaac.

Isaac, René, and the two Iroquois walked single file. As they neared the village stockade, Father Isaac sensed that the braves had

"Go back to the village!"
the taller brave commanded.

stopped. He turned around just in time to see one of the Iroquois throw off his blanket, uncovering a hidden tomahawk. The Iroquois swiftly brought the tomahawk down on René's head. "Jesus! Jesus! Jesus!" René cried. He staggered and then collapsed under the force of the blow.

Once again Father Isaac prayed the words of absolution over his dying friend. Then, seeing that René was still breathing, the Iroquois struck him a final time. Isaac fell to his knees, waiting for his own deathblow. But the Iroquois didn't stir. Isaac finally broke the silence. "Do whatever you want with me," he said. "I'm not afraid to die!"

12

Captivity

"Get up!" ordered the warrior who had attacked René. "We are not going to kill you now. You belong to another family."

At that one of the Iroquois from Isaac's longhouse came forward to claim him. As the two walked back to the house, Father Isaac's eyes filled with tears. It was September 29, the feast of Saint Michael, a fitting day for North America's first martyr.

After a sleepless night, Father Isaac rose before dawn. Slipping out of the village, he went to search for René's body. Some children were already outside. They knew where Isaac was going. "Look in the ravine," they told him.

Isaac did. And there he found René's body. He wept as he cradled it in his arms. Since he hadn't brought any tools for digging, Isaac decided to hide the body from the Iroquois until he could return to bury it. He gently laid it in a shallow stream and covered it with a mound of stones.

With a broken heart, Father Isaac returned to the longhouse.

On the following day Father Isaac was kept under surveillance and couldn't return to the stream. That afternoon a violent thunderstorm beat down on Ossernenon. The rain fell in torrents. Lightning streaked the sky. The storm raged on and off throughout the night. When the storm broke at sunrise, Isaac anxiously rushed back to the ravine. He waded through the icy stream, swollen by the rain, to the spot where he had hid René's body. It was gone! In sheer panic Isaac dove into the icy water. He dug into the wet mud with his hands. But he found nothing. *Some of the Iroquois have discovered the body and taken it away!* Father Isaac cried and prayed the psalms for the dead as he trudged back to the village. He felt so helpless...and so alone.

The autumn colors soon faded and the frost gave way to snow. The Iroquois journeyed to their winter hunting grounds, and Isaac went with them. Through the snow he carried bundles of food and supplies. He wore the only clothes he had: a thin shirt and torn pants. His moccasins were so worn that his feet bled continuously. He desperately longed to eat the meat that the braves brought in from the hunt but.... "I cannot eat this," he would tell the puzzled warriors. "It is meat that you've offered to your demon, Areskoui. I must not touch such food." Isaac had to be content with whatever crushed corn he could scrape from the bottom of the cooking pots.

In his suffering, Father Isaac turned to God. He set up a wooden cross in a hidden part of the forest. Whenever he could, he would slip away to pray there. "In front of this cross I spent most of the day with my God, whom I alone worshipped and loved in that forest," he later wrote. His sufferings, added to the fear of being tortured again, plunged Isaac into near despair. But God always came to his rescue. When he felt most alone Father Isaac heard a voice within him saying: *Serve God from love, not from fear. Do not worry about yourself.* This thought gave him the courage to go on.

When the Iroquois returned to Ossernenon after the winter hunt, Isaac kept busy visiting the longhouses in search of the sick and dying. He was able to baptize a few infants and adults who agreed to be baptized. He was allowed to travel to the villages of Andagaron and Tionontoguenk to care for the Huron and Algonquin prisoners.

Father Isaac encouraged them all and heard their confessions.

Isaac was also allowed to see and speak with William Coûture. They often talked together about René. They both agreed that he was a saint and a martyr. Father Isaac had proof, from the old chief who had ordered René's execution and from the child's mother, that René had been killed for tracing the sign of the cross on an Iroquois child. Isaac hoped to carry René's bones back to Quebec with him if he should ever be freed. He never believed the Iroquois' tale that René's body had been thrown into the river.

One day in March, some children called to Isaac: "Ondessonk! We have found the bones of the other Frenchman!"

Isaac raced across the field and climbed down into the ravine where the children claimed the bones were. He searched and prayed all day long, but found nothing. Finally, some older boys felt sorry for him and gave him a clue. "Ondessonk," they called, "you will find the bones higher on the slope, hidden under a clump of bushes."

Father Isaac didn't trust the boys completely, but for René he would try again. He climbed the muddy slope to the spot the boys pointed out. Tearing away the underbrush and branches, he uncovered the skull and bones of René! Isaac knelt and gently kissed each piece of bone, then carefully picked up the fragments. How precious they were! These bones were the relics of North America's first martyr.

Isaac was overjoyed! *I must bury the bones where they will be safe,* he thought. *If I ever do escape, I'll come back and retrieve them.*

Father Isaac found a spot at the base of a large tree. He dug a hole there, laid René's bones in it, and carefully covered them with earth.

Isaac walked back to the village with a much lighter heart. He had done all he could for his friend.

13

THE PLAN

In March of 1643, Father Isaac set out by canoe for the fishing grounds with the "aunt" in whose longhouse he stayed, her husband, and their grandson.

After traveling a whole day, they reached the Oiogué River. "Ondessonk!" his "aunt" whispered, "the cabins of the white men are only a few hours from here." Then she turned and walked away. *She's giving me an opportunity to escape,* Isaac realized with gratitude. *But it's not yet the time. The Lord will let me know when the time does come.*

Father Isaac was happy to be away from the noise of Ossernenon and the heckling of the Iroquois children and braves. In the quiet of the forest, he spent long hours in prayer. He even built a small cabin of bark hidden by a cluster of evergreen trees. And in this "chapel" he erected a cross.

One afternoon, Father Isaac's "aunt" came running frantically in search of him.

"Ondessonk! We must return to the village at once. The Algonquins are on the warpath, and they are nearby!"

"How do you know this?" Isaac questioned.

"Some braves have arrived to warn us. Hurry, Ondessonk!"

Father Isaac felt a strange sense of foreboding as he helped to break up camp and pack the fishing nets. The little group made the three-day canoe trip back to Ossernenon. As soon as they arrived, they learned the truth. The rumor about the Algonquin war party was a trick to get Ondessonk back to the village as soon as possible. It had been decided that he was to be tortured and burned!

As far as Father Isaac could gather from the women, the son of an elderly chief had reportedly been killed some time before. To offer a worthy sacrifice to the spirit of his son, the inconsolable chief had resolved that Ondessonk should be killed.

In vain did his "aunt" beg for Ondessonk's freedom. The blackrobe would die the following day—Good Friday. Isaac spent the night in prayer.

Early the next morning a messenger rushed into the village. "Your son is alive!" he told the chief. "He is on his way here with a band of warriors and twenty-two prisoners!" The whole village rushed through the gates to welcome the victorious warriors. In all the excitement Ondessonk was forgotten.

Only six of the prisoners were men. The others were women and children who were to be adopted by the Iroquois. The Algonquin captives were forced to run the gauntlet and led to the platform of torture. Father Isaac consoled them as best he could. Before their death, on Easter Sunday, he baptized them.

Following his own brush with death, Ondessonk's "aunt" was more anxious than ever to help him escape.

"Ondessonk, my nephew," she told him, "you must try to run away. Many braves are looking for an excuse to kill you."

Isaac nodded. He was beginning to realize that it might be best if he could escape. He was familiar with the ways of the Iroquois. He could speak their language fluently. It would be very important for him to share this knowledge with other Jesuit missionaries.

In May, Father Isaac had an opportunity to visit the Dutch settlement of Rensselaerswyck when his "aunt" decided to trade her furs there.

Isaac was very happy to mingle with Europeans again. He spoke with Arendt Van Corlaer, the director of the settlement, and found a good friend in the minister, Dominie Johannes Megapolensis. Van Corlaer bargained with the Iroquois again, but they refused his offer of a large ransom in exchange for Father Isaac's freedom.

After a few days, Ondessonk was led by his Iroquois guards back to imprisonment in Ossernenon.

By the summer of 1643, the Iroquois were stronger than ever. They terrorized the island of Montreal and forced the Hurons and Algonquins to flee north for safety.

Father Isaac's "aunt" decided to go on another fishing expedition.

"Ondessonk, my nephew," she confided, "before we fish we will go to the Dutch to trade."

Father Isaac sensed that she wanted to say more. He kept silent and waited for her to continue. "Ondessonk, you know your life is in danger here. I do not want to see you killed. Please...this time try to escape. There is nothing more you can do in our village."

True to her word, Isaac's "aunt" brought him with her when she went to trade at the

Dutch colony of Rensselaerswyck. Issac was treated very kindly by the colonists there. The Dutch were outraged that Father Isaac was enslaved by the Iroquois and suffered such torments at their hands. They admired this zealous French Jesuit.

In his free time, Father Isaac wrote to his superiors telling them of his situation and what he was able to accomplish with the Iroquois.

Then one afternoon, events took a sudden turn for the worse. Not long before the trading and fishing trip, Father Isaac had written a letter to warn the French of a future Iroquois attack. When the Iroquois learned of his role in their defeat, they were enraged. "Now you will be tortured and killed!" they threatened. The Iroquois braves beat him without mercy until he fell unconscious.

When Father Isaac came to again, he understood that this was no ordinary threat. He was now marked for death.

Arendt Van Corlaer couldn't just stand by and watch. "To allow you to return to Ossernenon, Isaac, would be to cooperate with your murder," he told the priest. "Something must be done! I have a plan," he continued in a low voice. "In a few days the ship in port will leave for Europe. I beg you to escape on it."

"But I would be endangering you and the Dutch," Father Isaac protested.

"We know how to deal with the Iroquois," Van Corlaer replied. "Think instead of this: what will be gained by your death?"

After much prayer and reflection, Isaac decided that he could in fact serve God better if he were free. He and Van Corlaer began to plan his escape.

14

ESCAPE!

"Father Isaac, you will find a rowboat by the river's edge," Van Corlaer instructed. "During the night, slip away from the Iroquois guards. Row out to the ship in the harbor. The captain has promised to bring you safely to Europe. Godspeed, my friend!"

Isaac walked slowly back to the barn where he would spend the night under the watch of the Iroquois braves. From his place in the corner he studied the building, mentally planning his escape.

At dusk, he stretched himself out on the dirt floor and pretended to sleep. Soon enough the Iroquois braves fell asleep. Noiselessly, Isaac got up and groped his way to the barn door. He pushed it open and squeezed through the narrow opening. He had only taken a few steps when he heard loud growls. Watchdogs suddenly jumped on him from all sides! One lunged at his legs and bit him. The Dutch owner of the barn rushed out of the house and beat the dogs off, but it was too late. By then all the Iroquois braves had rushed out into the yard.

The Dutchman was visibly upset to have ruined the escape. He quietly bandaged Isaac's wounded leg and sent him back to the barn. The Iroquois barred the doors and made Father Isaac lie down between them.

The hours ticked away. Isaac spent the rest of the night awake, his leg burning with pain. Worst of all, he felt that he had lost his only chance of escape.

Then, in the very early hours of the morning, Isaac thought he heard the door creaking. He sat up and strained to see. The braves still slept soundly. Isaac crept on his hands and knees to the barn door. A servant was unbarring it. Isaac motioned for him to tie up the watchdogs. The man obeyed, and Isaac slipped into the yard. It was still misty and gray outside.

With difficulty, Father Isaac climbed the fence and headed for the river. His leg throbbed and his heart pounded with fear. What if the Iroquois discovered he was gone?

He finally reached the riverbank. It was now almost dawn. There was the rowboat

Van Corlaer had promised. But one thing was desperately wrong—the tide was out, and the boat was stuck in the thick, black mud.

I'm too late! his mind frantically screamed as he pushed and tugged at the rowboat.

"Help! Help me!" he shouted to the ship in the harbor. There was no response.

On the other side of the river stood an Iroquois village that would be awakening any minute. He would soon be discovered....

Help, me Lord! Isaac prayed. *Please help me!* He grasped the boat once more and pushed with all his might. He felt it give. He threw his weight against it again and again. Inch by inch, the rowboat began to slide into the water. Finally, Isaac jumped in and began to row. Within minutes, the little boat thumped against the side of the ship. Father Isaac struggled up the rope ladder to the deck. The captain came out to greet him. "I can assure you of your safety while on board my ship, Father. But the Iroquois will soon come to search for you. You'll have to hide until we leave port."

Isaac nodded in agreement. "I understand, Captain."

The captain brought Isaac to a trapdoor leading to the hold of the ship. "You'll be safe down there, Father. I'll move a chest over the door to conceal it."

"Thank you for your kindness," Isaac murmured as he climbed into the dark space and hid among the cargo.

Back at the barn, the Iroquois braves awoke in anger. Ondessonk was gone! They searched the barn and the woods. They forced themselves into the homes of the Dutch looking for their prized prisoner.

"I am not hiding Ondessonk," Van Corlaer assured the braves, "but I will offer you gifts in exchange for your loss."

"We have no authority to accept the gifts of the Dutch in his place!" the warriors shouted back. "Ondessonk is a prisoner of the Iroquois nation!"

Van Corlaer decided it would be safer to remove Isaac from the ship. He would hide him in Rensselaerswyck until the fury of the native warriors had died down. For six weeks Father Isaac remained concealed. He spent most of this time in a cramped attic space with his wounded leg becoming more and more infected. The owner of the house, who wasn't too happy with his hidden guest, gave him very little to eat or drink. But Isaac's worst suffering was his constant fear that the Iroquois would punish the Dutch for his escape.

15

Christmas in France

Finally, at the orders of Arendt Van Corlaer, Father Isaac was smuggled onto a small ship that carried him down the Hudson River to New Amsterdam (the area that is now New York).

Father Isaac enjoyed his newfound freedom and the company of the Dutch who rejoiced over their own victory against the Iroquois. General Willem Kieft, the director of New Amsterdam, welcomed Isaac to his house and dressed him in a new black suit and cloak. The Dutch colonists looked upon Isaac with curiosity and admiration. His story was told in every home, over every teacup.

Toward the end of October, an old ship prepared to leave New Amsterdam for Europe.

"Father Isaac," General Kieft invited, "you're free to leave on this ship if you wish. I want to warn you, however, that it is hardly seaworthy."

"Sir, I place my life in God's hands," Isaac replied. "The Lord has spared me until now; I am confident he will bring me safely home."

Due to the small size of the ship, the voyage was rough. Sufferings were not lacking to Father Isaac. He slept on the upper deck among the coils of rope at the mercy of the waves and wind that swept over him.

After six weeks of treacherous sailing, the small vessel pulled into the English Channel. There a violent storm came up, forcing the captain to head for Falmouth, on the coast of England. To make matters worse, two pirate ships came along and began chasing the Dutch vessel, even firing their cannons at it. But the Dutch captain skillfully steered his ship and crew to safety.

Father Isaac had to remain on board when the ship finally docked because priests were outlawed in England at that time. Only a year earlier, in 1642, four priests had been executed there. One evening as he was sitting alone on deck, Isaac thought he heard footsteps. Suddenly a cold pistol pressed against his throat. "Quiet, or we'll kill you!" a voice snarled. Robbers had slipped on board! Anxious to see what treasures had been brought from the New World, they ransacked the ship's hold, searching the cargo and carrying off whatever they could...including Father Isaac's hat, coat, and cloak.

A few days later, Father Isaac boarded a small ship headed for Bordeaux, France.

"I assure you, Father, we will reach French soil by Christmas morning," the captain promised.

There will be Masses in the churches! Isaac thought with joy. *It's been seventeen months since I last went to confession, celebrated Mass, and received Holy Communion. Seventeen long months!*

The night of Christmas Eve Father Isaac couldn't sleep. Huddled on the ship's windy deck, he prayed. All during the night he prepared himself to receive the Sacraments of Penance and Holy Eucharist again. In his thoughts he traveled back to New France, to the chapel of Sainte Marie where his Jesuit brothers were celebrating midnight Mass with the native people. He wept because he would not be with the Hurons. But he *would* be in France. It all seemed like a dream!

Early Christmas morning the ship anchored near the shore of a small fishing village. A rowboat was lowered and Father Isaac quickly headed for the beach. France! He was home again in France!

He ran up to the first small cottage he spotted. Two fishermen smiled at him from the doorway. "Excuse me," Father Isaac ventured. "Is there a church nearby where I might attend Mass?"

The men were surprised at his strange French accent. "Yes," the older of the two replied. "Up the hill is a monastery. But if you're going to Mass, you should look more proper. Wait here. I have a better cap and scarf inside."

"Thank you, sir!" Isaac responded.

In a moment the man emerged from the cottage with the clothing. "Promise us you will return for breakfast after Mass, won't you?" he said. "After all, it is Christmas."

"I will return," Isaac said softly. "And I am very grateful to you."

Father Isaac practically ran up the hill leading to the monastery. The Christmas carols he loved as a boy played over and over in his heart. He entered the monastery chapel and looked for a priest to hear his confession. What a sense of peace he felt as he heard the words of absolution once again!

Then Mass began. When it was time for Holy Communion, Isaac knelt with the people at the altar rail. He felt such joy to receive the Eucharist again. Later on Father

Isaac wrote in his journal: "It seemed to me that it was then that I began to live once more. It was at that moment I tasted the joy of my freedom."

After Mass, Father Isaac slipped out of the church to avoid the curious but friendly stares of the villagers. He was warmly welcomed by the family back at the little cottage. "We have judged you to be an Irish refugee because of your peculiar French accent," the father began kindly, as Isaac eagerly ate the breakfast they had prepared. "Are we correct, my friend? What is your name?"

Isaac smiled. "A refugee I am, but Irish I am not. My name is Father Isaac Jogues, and I have just come from New France." He noticed his host's two little girls staring at his hands. "I was held captive by the Iroquois there for some time," he quietly added.

News of the missionary priest swept through the tiny village like wild fire. Monsieur Berson, a merchant from Rennes who was visiting a nearby town on business, offered to take Father Isaac back to the Jesuit house in that city. Isaac happily agreed. A few days later the two mounted their horses. Accompanied by promises of prayer and best wishes, Isaac began the 200-mile journey to Rennes.

16

HOMECOMING

Father Isaac was up before the sun on Tuesday, January 5. He was impatient to leave Monsieur Berson's house and return to his own Jesuit community.

By 5:30 A.M. he was knocking on the door of the College of Rennes. The brother porter opened it suspiciously. Isaac was quite a sight in his baggy coat and peasant cap.

"Please, Brother, I would like to see the Father Rector," Isaac requested.

"I'm very sorry, but Mass is just about to begin," the porter replied. "You may come inside and wait. Father will see you after Mass."

"Brother, please! I must see him now!" Father Isaac insisted. "I have important news about the Fathers in New France."

The porter was impressed by the urgency in Isaac's voice. And the mention of New France. It sounded important. The brother hurried to the sacristy and explained the situation to the rector. *The man may be in serious need,* the rector thought.

Removing his vestments, he walked briskly to the parlor. The room was still dark. The rector could see only the outline of the mysterious visitor.

"I understand you have come from New France?" he asked

"Yes, Father," Isaac responded.

"Do you know our Fathers there?"

"Yes, I do."

"Father Jean de Brébeuf?"

"Extremely well."

"And Father Isaac Jogues—do you know Father Jogues?"

"I know him even better, Father."

"We heard he was captured and tortured by the Iroquois." The rector's voice grew anxious now. "Do you bring news of Father Jogues?"

Isaac's eyes filled with tears and he dropped to his knees. "He is free, Father..." he answered in a hoarse whisper. "It is he who speaks with you now!"

The rector's hands trembled as he reached down to lift Isaac to his feet. The superior threw his arms around Father Isaac with joyous exclamations of welcome, then led him into a larger, well-lit room. Other priests and brothers, startled by the commotion, came rushing in to see what had happened.

"It is he who speaks with you now!"
Isaac whispered.

"Father Jogues has been returned to us! May God be praised!" Father Rector announced loudly.

The priests and brothers were so overcome that they hardly knew what to say. In great joy and gratitude they brought Father Isaac to the chapel where Father Rector celebrated Mass in thanksgiving for his safe return.

For days afterward, Father Isaac busied himself giving news of New France and learning all that had happened in France during his absence. He wrote letters to his superiors and to his mother, Madame Jogues, who believed he was dead.

But soon enough, Isaac began to feel uneasy. His brother Jesuits treated him with reverence and spoke about him as if he were a living martyr. Father Isaac didn't want praise; he wanted only to go unnoticed.

It was no better at his home in Orléans. His family and friends treated him like a canonized saint. From Orléans, Father Isaac was sent to Paris. There too he met the embarrassing praise of his friends and colleagues. Everyone seemed to know about him. Even the queen of France wanted to meet him!

Under obedience and with the greatest reluctance Father Isaac was escorted to the royal palace. Queen Anne received him with respect and kindness. She eagerly listened to the story of his capture, sufferings, and escape. She held his broken hands in her own while tears filled her eyes.

All of this honor and publicity troubled Isaac. He felt that he was not doing enough for the glory of God. How he longed to be back in the forests of New France!

Isaac repeatedly asked to return to New France. Father Filleau, his superior, understood what he was going through and allowed Father Isaac to leave for New France that spring.

Father Isaac was thrilled! He was only thirty-seven years old. He still had a good part of his life to spend in the Indian missions.

But one more thing had to be taken care of before Father Isaac left Europe. Because his hands had been so mutilated, he could not hold the Host at Mass in the usual way. He would need special permission from the Pope to be able to celebrate Mass. When Pope Urban VIII heard about Father Isaac's sufferings, he was greatly moved. He granted the needed permission at once. The Pope's answer reached Father Isaac in March. It had been twenty months since he had last celebrated Mass! When he finally approached the altar he felt as joyful as if he were celebrating his first Mass all over again. Now he was ready to return to New France!

17

Courageous Return

In the spring of 1644, Father Isaac set sail for New France. He would never see France again. After seven long weeks his ship pulled into the St. Lawrence Gulf. Isaac was overjoyed to see the native people again. *Thank you, Lord,* he prayed. *Thank you for bringing me back to where I really belong.*

In Quebec Father Isaac received a hearty welcome. His brother missionaries were as hungry for news from France as he was for their own news. But not all the news was good. "Father Isaac, five of the Iroquois nations are at war again," one of the priests sadly informed him. "We haven't been able to receive supplies for three years."

"Let me return to the Iroquois," Father Isaac begged the Jesuit superior in Quebec. "I know their language and their customs. I long to bring them the Gospel."

"We'll have to see, Isaac," the superior kindly replied. "Maybe later on. For the present you will be assigned to our mission in Montreal."

That September, after having refused to make peace with the Algonquins at a previous meeting, the Iroquois requested that another peace council be held at Three Rivers. Father Isaac traveled to the meeting with Father Jerome Lalemant. Besides many Hurons, some 400 Algonquin braves joined the council. After a week of speeches and discussions, a peace settlement was reached. The treaty included the Hurons, the Algonquins, the Iroquois, and the French. Governor Montmagny and the French leaders had their doubts about the treaty. So did Father Isaac. "Remember that the Iroquois Bear Clan is still hostile to the French," he warned.

Although he threw himself into his work among the Hurons in Montreal, Isaac longed to return to the Iroquois. His heart burned with a powerful desire to bring Jesus to this Indian nation. He believed that God willed him to live and die for the Iroquois people. They were always in his thoughts and prayers.

In February of 1646 the Iroquois sent representatives to Montreal. "Ondessonk, your aunt wishes you would return to her cabin once more," the spokesman told Father Isaac.

"The villagers of Ossernenon regret that you ran away. They now invite you to return."

Isaac was enthusiastic about the invitation. He immediately wrote to his superior to again offer himself as a missionary to the Iroquois. As he concluded his annual retreat in April, he received the reply he had so anxiously awaited: "Prepare yourself, Isaac. You will be sent to live with the Iroquois as soon as the opportunity arises."

In May another meeting was held with the Iroquois at Three Rivers. During the council, Father Isaac and Jean Bourdon, a French official, were accepted as ambassadors to the Iroquois. It was decided that they would make a trip to some of the main Iroquois villages to speak with the chiefs about keeping the peace treaty.

Father Isaac carefully packed in a small black chest the sacred vessels and vestments he would need to celebrate Mass. He prepared gifts of furs and jewelry for the Iroquois chiefs.

On May 16, the French and Algonquin ambassadors left Three Rivers for the country of the Iroquois. As they paddled south, Isaac shuddered at the remembrance of the tortures he had endured four years ago along this same route. *Lord,* he prayed, *have mercy on all who died then.*

After brief stops in the Iroquois village of Ossaragué and the Dutch settlement at Rensselaerswyck, the travelers continued on to Ossernenon. There Father Isaac was welcomed by the Iroquois—even by those who had tortured him.

Ondessonk's "aunt" was especially happy to see him again. Honatteniate, her grandson, had just been released from captivity by the French. He had told his grandmother about how well he had been treated as a French prisoner.

During his brief stay at Ossernenon, Father Isaac made a pilgrimage to the spot in the ravine where he had buried the bones of René Goupil. *My Lord,* he prayed, *may the sacrifice of René's life be the seed of faith for the Iroquois people.*

After a few days of meetings in the village of Tionontoguen, Isaac and Jean Bourdon stopped again at Ossernenon. Isaac learned that the Indians were suspicious about the locked chest he had left behind with his aunt. "Ondessonk," a brave cried in an accusing tone, "you are hiding an evil spirit in that box!"

Isaac smiled to himself. "I am not," he replied. "Come. See for yourselves." Opening the case, Father Isaac allowed the braves to examine all of its contents: the vestment and various items used at Mass. The braves seemed satisfied that Isaac was telling the truth. "I must return to Three Rivers for now," Father Isaac explained. "But I would like to leave the box here. I will need it if I ever come back to live with you."

"We will keep the black box here," the Iroquois promised, "until you return."

On Monday, September 24, three canoes slipped away from Three Rivers. Traveling with Father Isaac and Jean were the Huron braves who had agreed to spend the winter among the Iroquois.

After a few days on the water, the Hurons became uneasy. Father Isaac understood their fear. Everyone, both French and Indian, was wondering whether the Iroquois would really hold to their pledge of peace.

The Hurons' uneasiness grew greater. Although they saw no evidence to suggest it, they believed that the Iroquois had set a trap for them. In spite of Isaac's reassurances, they were convinced that this was true. The braves finally turned their canoes around and hurried back to the safety of their own villages. Only Otrihouré, the Huron ambassador, had the courage to continue the trip with Father Isaac and Jean.

When the three reached Lake Champlain, it was strangely quiet. In fact, there were no Iroquois in sight. September faded into October, and they paddled on.

On October 14, the three men pulled their canoe ashore and climbed the last trail leading to Ossernenon. Still there were no signs of the Iroquois.

Father Isaac's heart began to beat faster. He quickened his step. He was so happy to be returning to the Iroquois. With God's help, he would try to explain the Gospel to them.

Just then a group of Iroquois braves approached them on the trail. When Father Isaac called out in greeting, they disappeared among the trees. Isaac called out a second time. Suddenly angry cries filled the air. Iroquois braves streaked with war paint closed in on all sides, waving muskets and knives. Finally they had captured Ondessonk! This time he would not escape! The warriors leaped on Isaac, Jean, and Otrihouré. They tore off their clothes, beat them and dragged them into the village.

My God, help us! Father Isaac groaned within himself. *Everything is over. The Iroquois will attack and the French, Hurons, and Algonquins will be caught by surprise. How many will be killed!*

In the village some tried to beat the prisoners while others tried to protect them. Finally they were pushed into the longhouse of Father Isaac's "aunt." She bandaged Ondessonk's wounds and tried to explain what had happened since his last visit. "Nephew, the clans are divided," she said sadly. "The Wolf and Turtle clans want peace. The Bear clan does not. After you left there was a terrible sickness. Many people died. It spread from village to village. Some of the Huron prisoners told our people that the French brought the evil spirit. When it was time for harvest, our corn was destroyed by worms. We have no food for the winter. The sorcerers blamed everything on the black box you left behind. They said evil spirits escaped from it."

Now everything was beginning to make sense!

"Where is the box now, Aunt?" Isaac anxiously asked.

"The sorcerers dropped it into the river. It is gone."

19

The Darkest Night

All through the night of Wednesday, October 17, 1646 Issac, Jean and Otrihouré listened as the braves shouted threats of torture and death outside their longhouse. "An important council will be held in Tionontoguen tomorrow night," Father Isaac's Iroquois friends told him. "There the chiefs will decide your fate."

On Thursday, Father Isaac tried to reason with the chiefs, reminding them of the peace treaty they had made. But it did no good. That afternoon the Iroquois chiefs began their journey to Tionontoguen. Father Isaac and Jean spent the day in prayer.

Toward sunset, a young brave entered the longhouse. "Ondessonk, I come to invite you to a feast," he announced. "There are people who wish to eat and speak with you."

Isaac recognized the brave as a member of the Bear clan, which was hostile to him. He immediately suspected that something was wrong. But to refuse the invitation would be a serious insult. It would also show that he was a coward.

"I must first consult my family," Isaac calmly answered the brave.

"Nephew, I am worried," his "aunt" admitted. "If you must go, take my grandson, Honatteniate, with you. Your friend will stay here."

Father Isaac, Honatteniate, and the brave slipped into the cool evening air. The brave led them down the paths of the village. He stopped before a longhouse. Father Isaac could see the rough carvings of the clan's symbols on its doorposts. The young brave silently waited, his face showing no expression. Isaac pushed against the stiff animal skin that served as the cabin's door. In the semi-darkness he could see figures sitting around the fire. He stooped to enter. Honatteniate followed close behind. From behind the doorpost came the sudden swing of a tomahawk. Honatteniate tried to block the blow with his arm, but it was too late. Father Isaac fell to the floor.

Honatteniate ran from the longhouse as the braves began to celebrate. They had killed Ondessonk, the great sorcerer! Now they would be free from the evil spirits.

*Isaac pushed against the animal skin and
stooped to enter.*

On hearing the news, Ondessonk's "aunt" rushed to the scene. "You have killed one of my family!" she wailed. "You did not wait for the decision of the chiefs!"

The Bear clan braves cut off Father Isaac's head and mounted it on the village palisade, facing the land of the French.

The Wolf clan hid Jean in their longhouse while the rebel Indians surrounded it, calling for the family to surrender him. "We will kill all the French!" they threatened.

All through the night Jean waited and prayed. He felt alone and afraid. But he had confessed his sins and received absolution from Father Isaac that morning. Jean knew that he was prepared to die.

After some time, the village grew quiet. Jean thought about Isaac. *Father Isaac is a martyr,* he reasoned. *I must find and bury his body. It is my duty.*

Jean crept out of the longhouse, never noticing the braves who were waiting in the darkness. Before he could even cry out, a tomahawk brought him to the ground. The braves placed his head next to Ondessonk's on the palisade. They then cast the martyrs' bodies into the Mohawk River.

Sunrise came. Just as news of the young Frenchman's death was racing through the village, a messenger arrived from Tionontoguen. "I bring the Great Council's decision," he announced. "The Frenchmen are to be freed and escorted safely back to Three Rivers!"

The people were in an uproar over this news. The messenger ran back to Tionontoguen to report the murders. The assembled chiefs denounced what had taken place. They were humiliated by the treachery of the act. Never again would the Iroquois' word be trusted.

Otrihouré, the Huron ambassador, was sent back to Three Rivers to assure Governor Montmagny that the murder of Ondessonk had been a mistake. But Otrihouré himself was killed before he ever reached the settlement.

The chiefs were so ashamed of the murders that they commanded their people to keep everything a secret. But the news reached Rensselaerswyck. The Dutch were horrified. They had always admired and respected Father Isaac. Ondessonk's "aunt" later smuggled down to Rensselaerswyck whatever personal belongings of Father Isaac and Jean she had been able to save.

20

THE SEED

Throughout the winter there were more signs that the Iroquois were breaking the peace treaty. In Montreal, Father Le Jeune was worried about Father Isaac and Jean. *It's strange that they haven't sent us any word after all this time,* he mused.

In June, the Jesuits finally received news from a Huron who had escaped from the Iroquois. It confirmed what they already sensed in their hearts: Father Isaac and Jean had been killed.

That September, the French and Algonquins managed to overcome an Iroquois war party. An Iroquois warrior was taken prisoner. He was questioned and identified by some Hurons who had escaped from the Iroquois as the one who had killed Ondessonk. Although he never actually confessed, it was generally believed that he had committed the crime. At Quebec this Iroquois brave listened to the blackrobes. He was sincerely sorry for what he had done and asked God's pardon. He was eventually baptized...and given the new name Isaac Jogues.

Honatteniate, the grandson of Father Isaac's "aunt," asked to live with the French. Later, he was sent to France. In Paris he came down with a terrible fever. Honatteniate's greatest desire came true when he was finally baptized just a half hour before his death.

In 1649, five more blackrobes were struck down by the warring Iroquois. They were Fathers Jean de Brébeuf, Antoine Daniel, Charles Garnier, Noël Chabanel, and Gabriel Lalemant. Together with Father Isaac Jogues, René Goupil, and Jean de La Lande, these Jesuit martyrs gave up their lives for the salvation of the Native American people.

On June 29, 1930, Pope Pius XI canonized all eight of the martyrs. We celebrate their feast day every October 19. Through their heroic sacrifice, Saint Isaac and the other martyrs planted the precious seed of the Christian faith in North America. And it was a seed that grew.... Those Native Americans, especially the Hurons, who had become Christians spread the Good News of Jesus throughout large areas of New France and what is now New York State.

In 1656, just one generation after the death of the martyrs, in the very village of Ossernenon where Father Isaac and Jean had been killed, Kateri Tekakwitha was born. Against the wishes of her family and friends, this young Mohawk woman heroically embraced the Catholic faith. She felt in her heart the same flame of love that had burned so strongly in the hearts of Saint Isaac and his fellow missionaries. Kateri became an example of goodness and kindness to all. Today the Church honors her as Blessed Kateri Tekakwitha. One day, when *she* is canonized, Kateri will become the very first Native North American saint.

PRAYER

Saint Isaac, your love for Jesus was so great that you wanted all people to know and love him too. You gave up everything *you had—even your life—to bring the Good News of Jesus to the Native peoples of North America.*

Help me to grow in love each day. Help me to imitate Jesus and to lead others to him just as you did. Ask God to give me the courage I need to live my Catholic faith, especially when I have to face problems or things that make me suffer. I want to believe, hope, and love as you did. Pray for me, Saint Isaac. Amen.

GLOSSARY

1. **Absolution**—the act by which a priest forgives a person's sins in the Sacrament of Penance.

2. **Ambush**—to attack someone from a hiding place; the name given to a surprise attack.

3. **Blessed Sacrament**—another name for the Holy Eucharist, the real Body and Blood of the risen Jesus present under the appearances of bread and wine at Mass. The name Blessed Sacrament is especially used to refer to the Holy Eucharist kept, in the form of consecrated hosts, in the tabernacle.

4. **Chasuble**—the outer vestment worn by a priest at Mass. The color of the chasuble changes according to the seasons of the liturgical year.

5. **Chrism**—a special oil mixed with balsam (a fragrant substance found in certain trees) that is usually blessed by the bishop on Holy Thursday. Chrism is used in the celebration of the Sacraments of

Baptism, Confirmation, and Holy Orders and at the consecration of bishops. It is also used to *consecrate,* or set apart for holy use, churches, altars, chalices, and patens, and to bless the water used at baptism.

6. **Diocesan priest**—any priest who is not a member of a religious order but lives and works in a specific diocese in obedience to his bishop.

7. **Influenza**—a severe, infectious disease that affects the respiratory tract and is contagious.

8. **Jesuit**—a priest or brother belonging to the religious order founded by Saint Ignatius of Loyola. This order's official name is the Society of Jesus.

9. **Master of novices**—the priest or brother who teaches and guides new members who are preparing to make their vows in a religious order.

10. **Musket**—a type of long gun that was used before the invention of the rifle.

11. **Novitiate**—a special training period for those preparing to become religious priests, brothers, or sisters. The actual building where this instruction takes place is also called the novitiate.

12. **Ordination**—the ceremony during which a man receives the Sacrament of Holy Orders. A man may be ordained a deacon, a priest, or a bishop.

13. **Palisade**—a kind of fence made of pointed wooden posts and used to protect a village from attack.

14. **Porter**—in some male religious communities the name given to the person who answers the door and greets visitors.

15. **Prostrate**—to lie in a facedown position or to bow very low.

16. **Ravine**—a narrow, deep valley, especially one formed by running water.

17. **Stole**—the band of cloth which a priest or bishop wears around his neck during the celebration of Mass and the administration of the sacraments. (A deacon also uses a stole on these occasions, but it is worn across the left shoulder.)

18. **Theology**—the study of God and his relations with the created universe.

19. **Vow**—an important promise freely made to God. Members of religious communities usually make vows of chastity, poverty, and obedience.

Daughters of St. Paul

| We Pray | We Preach | We Praise |

Centering our lives on Jesus, Way, Truth, Life

Witnessing to the joy of living totally for Jesus

Sharing Jesus with people through various forms of media: books, music, video, & multimedia

If you would like more information on following Jesus and spreading His Gospel

as a Daughter of St. Paul…

contact:

Vocation Director
Daughters of St. Paul
50 Saint Pauls Avenue
Boston, MA 02130-3491
(617) 522-8911
e-mail: vocations@pauline.org
or visit www.pauline.org

Pauline
BOOKS & MEDIA

The Daughters of St. Paul operate book and media centers at the following addresses. Visit, call or write the one nearest you today, or find us on the World Wide Web, www.pauline.org

CALIFORNIA
3908 Sepulveda Blvd., Culver City, CA 90230; 310-397-8676
5945 Balboa Ave., San Diego, CA 92111; 858-565-9181
46 Geary Street, San Francisco, CA 94108; 415-781-5180

FLORIDA
145 S.W. 107th Ave., Miami, FL 33174; 305-559-6715

HAWAII
1143 Bishop Street, Honolulu, HI 96813; 808-521-2731
Neighbor Islands call: 800-259-8463

ILLINOIS
172 N. Michigan Ave., Chicago, IL 60601; 312-346-4228

LOUISIANA
4403 Veterans Blvd., Metairie, LA 70006; 504-887-7631

MASSACHUSETTS
Rte. 1, 885 Providence Hwy., Dedham, MA 02026; 781-326-5385

MISSOURI
9804 Watson Rd., St. Louis, MO 63126; 314-965-3512

NEW JERSEY
561 U.S. Route 1, Wick Plaza, Edison, NJ 08817; 732-572-1200

NEW YORK
150 East 52nd Street, New York, NY 10022; 212-754-1110
78 Fort Place, Staten Island, NY 10301; 718-447-5071

OHIO
2105 Ontario Street (at Prospect Ave.), Cleveland, OH 44115; 216-621-9427

PENNSYLVANIA
9171-A Roosevelt Blvd., Philadelphia, PA 19114; 215-676-9494

SOUTH CAROLINA
243 King Street, Charleston, SC 29401; 843-577-0175

TENNESSEE
4811 Poplar Ave., Memphis, TN 38117; 901-761-2987

TEXAS
114 Main Plaza, San Antonio, TX 78205; 210-224-8101

VIRGINIA
1025 King Street, Alexandria, VA 22314; 703-549-3806

CANADA
3022 Dufferin Street, Toronto, Ontario, Canada M6B 3T5; 416-781-9131
1155 Yonge Street, Toronto, Ontario, Canada M4T 1W2; 416-934-3440

¡También somos su fuente para libros, videos y música en español!